DREAMS
AROUND THE WORLD

TAKASHI OWAKI

ONE PEACE BOOKS

Published by One Peace Books, Inc. in 2012
Originally published in Japan as *Dreams* by Sanctuary Books in 2010

Translated by Robert McGuire
Edited by Erin Canning
Cover design and layout by Shimpachi Inoue
Special thanks to Julianne Neville and L.J. Ruell

ISBN: 978-1-935548-11-9

First Edition

Printed in China

One Peace Books
43-32 22nd Street, Suite #204
Long Island City, NY 11101
www.onepeacebooks.com

Distribution by SCB Distributors
15608 South New Century Drive
Gardena, CA 90248
www.scbdistributors.com

Dear Reader,

My name is Takashi, and I am a photographer who lives in Tokyo, Japan.

Over the course of three years, I traveled to fifty-five countries on six different continents. During my travels, I met many children and asked them the same question: "What do you want to be when you grow up?" Of course, I heard a lot of different answers!

In this book, I have included the dreams of thirteen children, along with my stories of meeting each child. I hope you learn a little about each of them while also discovering that you have things in common, despite coming from very different places. Most importantly, I hope you're inspired to think about your own dreams.

Enjoy!

Takashi Owaki

name		age
	Mengue	*5*

Mengue's dream is to be a...

DANCER

I meet Mengue on the day of the Islamic festival known as Tabaski. On this special day, the young girls have their hair braided by their mothers or older sisters and dress up. After dinner, they visit houses in the neighborhood to receive candy and small monetary gifts. Mengue dreams of being a dancer because dancing makes her happy.

Dancing!

A baobab tree in Touba

Mengue with her cousins

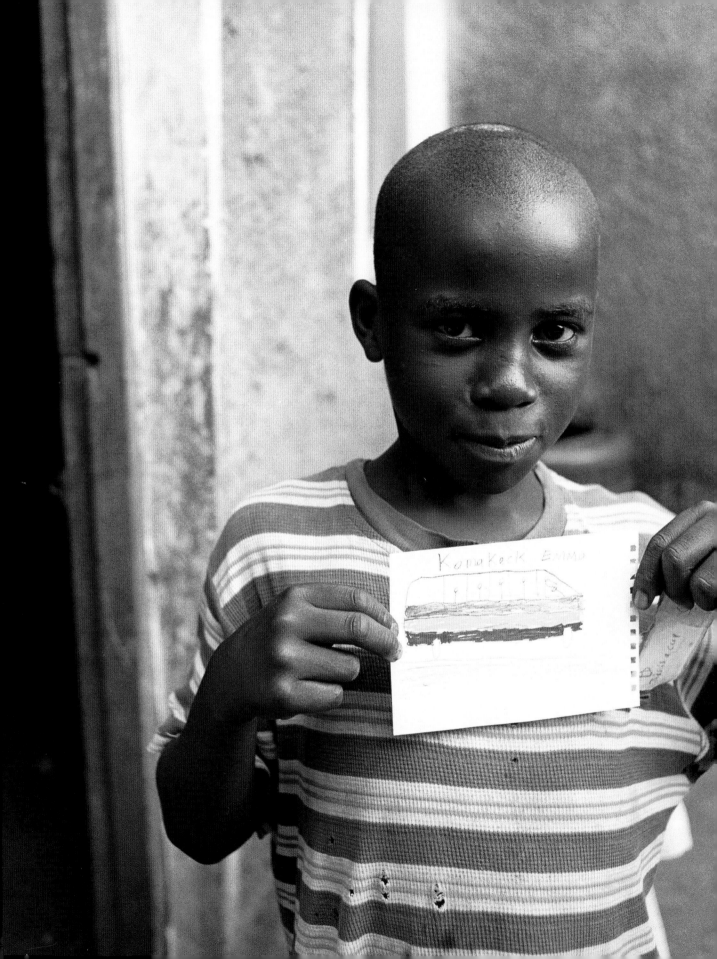

name	Emma	age	8

Emma's dream is to be a...

TAXI DRIVER

I meet Emma at an airfield where children are playing soccer. The airfield sits in the shadow of Tororo Rock. Most of the children dream of being either taxi drivers or soccer players. Taxi drivers drive mini-buses called *matatu*. Emma draws a matatu that shares the colors of the Ugandan flag.

The airfield near Tororo Rock

Emma with his siblings

Taking a walk through Tororo

Philippines
Manila

name		age
	Angelica	*6*

Angelica's dream is to be a...

DOCTOR

I meet Angelica on a hot, sunny day in the Las Piñas neighborhood of Manila. She and her friends are energetically playing in an alleyway covered with graffiti. They play hide-and-seek, dance in a circle, and draw pictures. Angelica dreams of being a doctor, so she can help those in need.

Playing hide-and-seek!

Friends!

Dancing!

name		age
	Udayakumar	6

Udayakumar's dream is to be a...

PILOT

I meet Udayakumar at an Indian restaurant his father runs. His father moved to Malaysia from India twenty years ago. The restaurant specializes in dishes made with the large leaves of bananas. While Udayakumar's sister, Nandini, helps their mother at the cash register, he tries to get a restaurant employee to play with him. Udayakumar dreams of becoming a pilot, so he can visit many countries.

Udayakumar with his family

Indian food with banana leaves

Having fun with the staff!

**China
Tianjin**

name		age
	Ang	7

Ang's dream is to be a...

KUNG-FU MASTER

I meet Ang in a public square where he is practicing kung fu with a group of kids. They are diligently following instructions from their teacher, a former gymnast. They work on their flexibility and strength and practice poses. Ang is a serious student, and his poses are very good. The older girls in the class think he is cute. Ang dreams of being a kung-fu master like Bruce Lee.

And another pose!

Ang's kung-fu class

Striking a pose!

name		age
	Cosmo	*4*

Cosmo's dream is to be a...

HOUSE BUILDER

I meet Cosmo in Regent's Park, a Royal Park that was founded by Henry VIII. He and his brother are playing in a large hammock strung between two trees. Cosmo and his family visit the park daily. Cosmo especially likes to play in the tree house near the lake. He dreams of being a house builder, so he can build a tree house of his own.

Cosmo with his family

Playing in the hammock!

Climbing to the tree house!

names		ages
	Roksanka (left) and Emilia (right)	6

Roksanka's dream is to be a...

PRINCESS

Emilia's dream is to be a...

BALLERINA

I meet Roksanka and Emilia at a ballet school located in the center of the beautiful city of Gliwice. Poland is the proud birthplace of the composer Frédéric Chopin, so classical music and ballet are a part of everday life here. Children learn to dance from an early age, including Roksanka and Emilia, two prima ballerinas.

Discussing a ballet technique!

Roksanka and Emilia's classmates

name		age
	Sara	7

Sara's dream is to be a...

JOCKEY

I meet Sara in a quiet suburb that is located on Lake Päijänne, the second largest lake in Finland. She and her siblings are playing in front of the new house built by their father. Sara and her family are planning to go for a bike ride around the lake later in the afternoon. Sara dreams of being a jockey and loves when her father takes her horseback riding.

Sara with her mother

A view of Lake Päijänne

Getting ready for a bike ride!

Russia
Moscow

name		age
	Yolka	*7*

Yolka's dream is to be a...

WRITER

I meet Yolka at the hostel where her mother works. She comes here every day after school. Yolka dreams of being a writer in New York. She once lived in the United States and speaks English very well. When I ask her why she would like to live in New York, she replies, "America is friendly, and their president is a good leader."

Hanging out at the hostel!

Getting a ride from mom!

Yolka with her grandmother

name		age
	Armando	*8*

Armando's dream is to be a...

CLOWN

I meet Armando at the traveling circus that his family helps run. They perform throughout Mexico all year long. Today the big top is being pitched. Armando has the important job of taking care of the llamas and donkeys. Armando is very nimble and would make a good tightrope walker. He dreams of being a clown, so he can make people laugh.

Clowning around!

The big top

Cartwheel!

name		age
	Rafaella	8

Rafaella's dream is to be a...

POLICE OFFICER

I meet Rafaella at a street stand where she is helping her mother sell sausages. Though Rafaella's family shares a small home with two other families, they are very happy. Rafaella likes fashion and enjoys changing her outfit a few times a day. She dreams of being a police officer, so she can clean up the streets of her unsafe city.

Rafaella's mother and neighbors

A street in Port-au-Prince

Friends!

name		age
	Diego	5

Diego's dream is to be a...

GELATO SHOP OWNER

I meet Diego in San Telmo, one of the oldest neighborhoods in Buenos Aires. He has just finished kindergarten for the day and meets his father and brother, Matisse, outside of the school. Diego's curly hair brings to mind the composer Johann Sebastian Bach. Diego dreams of owning a gelato shop, so he can eat a lot of his favorite treat.

School's out!

Diego with his family

Hanging out after school!

Brazil
São Gonçalo do Sapucai

name		age
	Rayane	*8*

Rayane's dream is to be a...

TEACHER

I meet Rayane at her grandfather's house. She and many of her relatives are getting ready to parade in a festival. The men and boys play the drums while the women and girls dance the samba, a traditional dance. They show their national pride by wearing matching uniforms that are the colors of the Brazilian flag. Rayane is a good samba dancer.

Drum practice

Rayane with her sister and cousins

Samba dancing!

North America

Armando

Rafaella

South America

Rayane

Diego

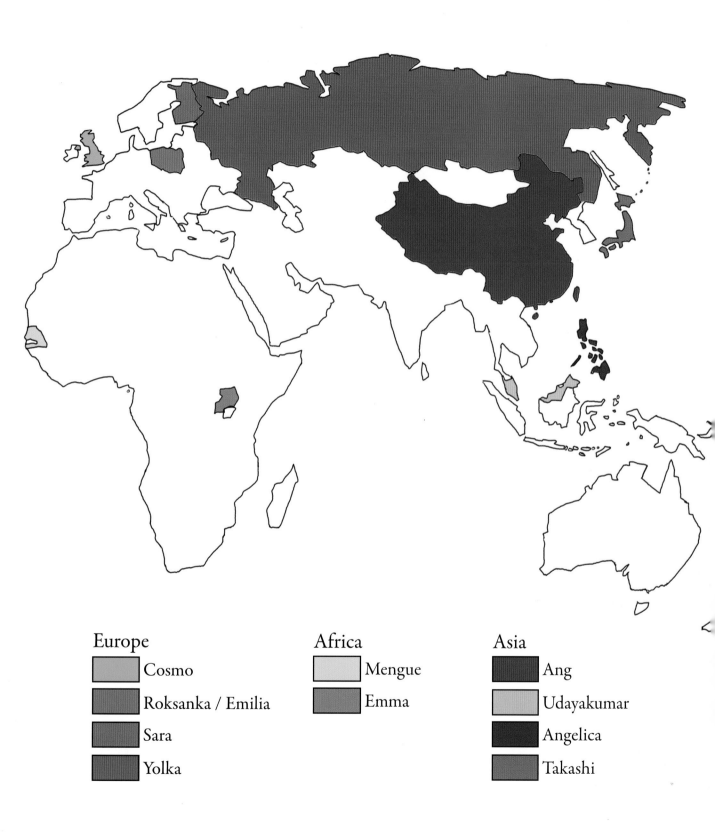

Europe
Cosmo
Roksanka / Emilia
Sara
Yolka

Africa
Mengue
Emma

Asia
Ang
Udayakumar
Angelica
Takashi

WHAT DO YOU WANT TO BE WHEN YOU GROW UP?